# REIGNING CHAMPIONS

## OVERCOMING LUST ADDICTION

### Joel Ishler

WESTBOW
PRESS
A DIVISION OF THOMAS NELSON

ISBN: 978-1-4497-7619-0 (sc)
ISBN: 978-1-4497-7618-3 (e)

Library of Congress Control Number: 2012921472

WestBow Press books may be ordered through booksellers or by contacting:
WestBow Press
A Division of Thomas Nelson
1663 Liberty Drive
Bloomington, IN 47403
www.westbowpress.com
1-(866) 928-1240

Unless otherwise noted, all scripture quoted is from the
New King James Version of the Holy Bible.

Printed in the United States of America

WestBow Press rev. date: 11/30/2012

# Contents

# ACKNOWLEDGEMENTS

The author is deeply grateful for the contributions, support, encouragement, and editorial help offered by his wife, Elsa, his pastor, Drew Koen, his mother, Eilene Ishler, his former mentor, Eric Williams, and the wonderful staff at Westbow Press. This book would not have gotten across the finish line without you. Thank you.

# ONE

# YOUR ENEMY'S GAME PLAN

## AN ILLICIT AFFAIR

Successful teams in sports study how their opponents play on the field. Why? If they can anticipate the other team's strategy, then they can change the outcome of the game.

I believe you're reading this because you are ready to stop losing to lust and start being a winner. I promise you: *if* you follow the strategies I give you with all of your heart, you *can* win this battle.

Lust has dominated men for far too long, but what I've learned is that lust has a game plan. It runs the same plays every game. It is predictable. Therefore, as we learn its line of attack, we will be able to see how to counteract it and turn the tables on lust.

Let me tell you a story that illustrates the approach lust takes. A world famous political leader decided to take a rest from the battlefield during wartime and went out for a walk one evening.

While he was on his balcony, he saw a gorgeous woman taking a bath with nothing on. He took a second look. Then he found out who this bathing beauty was.

When he found out she was a married woman he didn't stop pursuing her. Instead, he arranged for an introduction with her and the two of them had sex.

The woman sent the politician word that she was pregnant and, rather than owning up to his wrong- doing, he used his authority to arrange for her husband to be killed. The political leader then married the woman that he had had the illicit affair with—all to cover up his guilt and indiscretion.

> *"...I promise you: if you follow the strategies I give you with all of your heart, you can win this fight."*

The story, as you may have guessed, is that of King David and Bathsheba. You can read about it in 2 Samuel 11-12. What is my point in telling you this story? To show you that lust is never satisfied.

Lust starts with a look, lingers into a fantasy, and soon becomes an obsession that will stop at nothing to get what it wants. This story reveals the pattern of lust. Lust wants you to believe it is your buddy, and that it just wants to show you a good time. The truth is that, if you allow it go unchecked, it will destroy you.

I know this from experience—because, from the time I was twelve years old, I got hooked on lust and became a porno addict. I spun a web of lies to everyone dear to me in order to keep myself looking as pure as the driven snow. I jeopardized my job to "borrow" adult videos from a retail merchandise store. In short, lust was my "drug", and I was hooked.

I found lust to be all-consuming. It took over my thoughts, my schedule, my energy, my relationships, and it almost took my life. I was so desperate for change that I became suicidal, thinking death was the only way for me to be free.

However, I found another way out, and so can you. You don't have to live with the problem. That is another sly strategy our Enemy will want you to believe: that everyone does it, so you should just accept your problem rather than look for a way to overcome it. But you *can* and *will* overcome it, as long as you don't give up. You can either conquer lust, or you can continue to allow lust to conquer you. It's your choice.

I won't give you a quick-fix formula to follow from my life, because I don't believe that would be effective in seeing results that last. Instead, I will give you *principles* that work when you allow them to change your approach to the problem. I have come to see myself differently, and the problem differently—that is the key to seeing real change.

## Lust's Playbook

Your enemy, lust, knows that the two main ways of getting to your heart are your eyes and your ears. The first step in the temptation we all face as men is what we look at. Now I believe that it is impossible not to notice an attractive woman. Yet the truth is that you don't have to *keep* looking. You are in control of what you look at and listen to. You *can* control what you focus on, and what you tune into.

The truth is that as men, we are visually motivated. This is why most men love action movies—because there are lots of impressive visuals to feast our eyes on.

In fact, we live in a society that constantly bombards us with images. Advertisers know how to get you hooked on their products: they need to grab your eyes.

Leading fashion magazines train women from an early age to believe that if they want to get your attention, they need to make their bodies as appealing as possible.

Therefore, they lower the neckline of their blouses, raise the hemlines of their skirts, tighten the fit of their clothes, etc. But I can assure you that no self-respecting woman wants to get involved with a man who is looking at her like she's just "eye candy."

The problem is that, if we do not control what we focus on, our whole lives will spiral out of control. Our eyes give everyone a window into what is really going on in our souls.

Secondly, we are suckers for flattery. The compliments we receive from women can be a huge tug on our heart. We love for women to feed our ego. The truth we want to believe their hype more than they do. It is a blurry boundary between flattery and flirtation, but my point is that we can be greatly influenced—and even led astray—by what we listen to. Many people who have had affairs will agree with me.

What you focus on—through images and words—determine what you think about. This is the second step in the strategy of lust: to get a hold of your mind.

Your imagination becomes a thrill ride of fantasies involving who your eyes are getting loaded up with. Soon the rollercoaster of "dirty thoughts" takes you on twists and turns of new ideas and possibilities.

### "You can either conquer lust, or you can continue to allow lust to conquer you."

But what starts off as so exciting will make you feel like you want to throw up by the time lust is done. This is because you think you are just in for a good time, but you soon realize you are not in control. Lust is. You are helplessly strapped in for the trip, and you are being taken places you don't want to go. You'll eventually be begging to get off this crazy ride, vowing that you will never get on it again.

Our imagination is powerful, and *can* be a great help to us in life. However, lust wants to use your imagination to distract you from what you should be thinking about. In lust, your mind puts so much energy into your fantasy life that it has nothing left for what's real.

## "No woman can live up to the 'perfect' fantasy you have created."

The sexual fantasies become so "fantastic" that real life can't possibly compete, and neither can real women. No woman can live up to the "perfect" fantasy you have created. The obvious reality is that there are no perfect people. This is how lust destroys the relationships that you are in, or keeps you from even getting into one.

Real relationships require work. They aren't nearly as easy to maintain and improve upon as a picture-perfect fantasy with your ideal physical type. You won't know how to relate to women if you only see them as bodies to have sexual fantasies about.

As an aside, let me just say this: if you refuse to settle for the easy way out in your romance, you'll experience so much more in life than you ever could have otherwise imagined possible. When you invest in your relationship with the opposite sex, then the mutual need for "oneness" is realized. It happens as you improve communication and learn to understand one another.

The third play lust makes for us as men is daring us to act on the fantasies we are entertaining. The urges turn into self-gratification—meaning masturbation, but that's just the start.

Many men have confided in me that they feel compelled to act out the fantasies they have been playing in their head—with or *without* the consent of the other person. It is this burning desire to fulfill this urge that motivates other men to rape, kidnap, and even murder other people.

The lust addiction is just like a drug. As you give into it more and more, you aren't satisfied with just a look; you are driven to fantasy. You move from "soft" to "hard" porn as you crave bigger and bigger "highs" of ecstasy. Soon fantasies are no longer enough, and you have to act on the desires that have you so preoccupied.

Just like a drug, lust convinces you to cover up your addiction at all costs. Think about it: When was the last time you saw a porno magazine on someone's living room coffee table? Men *hide* them because they know what they are doing is wrong. Whether we admit it or not, our actions show that we are ashamed of our behavior.

Soon you start lying to protect your double life, and the lies get bigger and bigger. When your mom finds the lingerie pictures you used to masturbate to, you tell a lie and say that they are your sister's. If your sister finds a copy of *Hustler* under your bed, you claim it was left there by aliens. I'm exaggerating, of course, but you see my point.

Then paranoia sets in as you try to keep up your secret life. You become convinced that someone will discover the truth about your "little problem." You hear people snickering in the hallway at school or at work, and you're sure that they're laughing about your issues.

Fear of being found out by those you care about eventually begins to torment you. It cuts you off from the very people who want to help you because you don't want to let them down and admit your weakness. Before you know it, lust has made your life a living hell.

Sound familiar? You see, I know what you're going through because I've been there. Even though most guys don't believe me when I tell them this, it's still true: I've been *clean* for eight years.

I'm serious: eight entire years. I haven't masturbated or entertained fantasies about anyone—except my wife, for that long. Life is *so* much better now as a result of the freedom that I have found.

## REIGNING CHAMPIONS

Please realize that I'm just like you. I'm convinced that *you* can have this same victory over lust too. I know that what I teach you will give you the breakthrough you want so badly *if* you apply it diligently.

This is why I want to help you. I don't want you to go through the agony and depression that I went through for so long, as I became more and more desperate for help. I don't want to see you become a slave to your sexual desires and remain helpless. You can be truly free.

Don't believe the lies that I believed for so long... "You'll never change." "Every guy is doing it, so that makes it okay." "As long as you aren't hurting anyone, what's the big deal?"

Once you know the truth, the truth will *make* you free.

## JOIN THE TEAM

Are you ready to join the winning team? If so, if you are truly ready—I mean *hungry* with every fiber of your being for victory over lust, then let's get to it. You have already taken the first step in buying this book to study. In my eyes, that makes you a "number one draft pick."

Now it's time for spring training. I'm going to put you through boot camp. It's going to be intense. It's going to get tough. But stick with me, and you too, will be a reigning champion.

You already have a big advantage over your opponent which is lust. You can always recognize its strategy, because it's the same *every time*. You can then stop those strategies from succeeding *every time-* if you use the tools that I give you.

Remember what we have learned. Lust *starts* with a lingering look at a woman or a flattering remark from a woman that grabs your attention.

## "Once you know the truth, the truth will make you free."

Next, it *moves* into the imagination until it dominates your thinking. Finally, it *urges* you to act out the fantasies that have you so preoccupied.

Let me assure of this: you are not alone in this fight. Lust wants us to be isolated, to think that what we are going through is unusual. I have found a very safe place in being honest with other men whom I trust, about my challenges and temptations.

This accountability will help develop healthy friendships with other men. You need to join with other men who see how important this victory over lust is. Just like the game of tug-of-war where we all need to pull together if we're going to become champions. In the final chapter of this book you'll find information on how to do just that.

# Let's Review

1.  Why do successful teams in sports study their opponents' plays on the field?

2.  Do you agree that lust is all-consuming? Why or why not?

3.  How has lust affected your life?

4.  What are the two main entryways into our heart?

5.  What you focus on determines what? (See page five.)

6.  How can imagination be a help to a romantic relationship? How can it hurt the relationship?

7.  Has lust tempted you to do things that shocked you? If so, would you share them with the group?

8.  How is lust a lot like a drug?

9.  What should you be hungry for if you are going to experience victory over lust?

10. Why is it important to join this group you've started and become part of a team?

## NOTES:

_____

_____

_____

_____

_____

_____

_____

_____

_____

_____

_____

_____

_____

_____

_____

_____

_____

_____

_____

_____

_____

_____

_____

_____

_____

_____

# TWO

# THE MIRROR IMAGE

## MEET YOUR HEAD COACH

Let's get straight to the heart of the issue of overcoming lust. How do you see yourself? What is your self-image?

Do you realize that this may be the *biggest* problem we can experience? How we see ourselves determines whether or not we overcome the problem of lust. How we see ourselves even determines where we'll end up in life.

I intend to show you that you need to exchange your image of yourself for God's image of you. Yes. *God.* He has designed us perfectly, but if we don't follow His instructions, we can't expect our lives to work right.

### *"How we see ourselves determines whether or not we overcome the problem of lust."*

Let me explain what I mean. Think of receiving the gift of a remote control car for Christmas as a kid.

*Most boys* tend to put the batteries in and start playing with it immediately. However, there's a problem: the car is in pieces. It needs to be carefully assembled and with the right battery put in, etc. Most boys will try to figure it out themselves, not even following the instructions that are included with the toy *until* they get stuck and can't figure out what to do.

This is not how we should live life. We should *start* with God's instructions and not use them as a last resort. He is the best One to help us not only put our lives together, but also to hold our lives together. He empowers us to live our lives to the fullest.

If you have trouble believing that...I am convinced it is only because you have the wrong image of God. Western society has bought and sold the idea that God is a cruel judge who loves to see us suffer. The world wants you to believe that He causes every trouble and tragedy. I used to think the same thing.

Now that I have gotten to know who God really is through the Bible, I guarantee that nothing could be further from the truth. He cares about us more than we will ever understand. He wants us to have the best lives imaginable, and He has given us the keys we need to have Heaven on earth.

However, He knows that our "issues" (which is just a modern slang for what the Bible calls "*sin*") with things like lust will keep us from experiencing that kind of life.

## Broken Pieces

Let's go back to the beginning and discover where things went wrong so we can understand how to make it right.

*Then God said, "Let Us make man in Our image, according to Our likeness… So God created man in His own image; in the image of God He created him; male and female He created them.* (Genesis 1:26, 27)

God originally created mankind to be in His image. Think for a moment about a mirror. A mirror is something designed to reflect our image so we can see what we look like, right? Well, we were designed to be the mirror image of God.

That is who we are. You and I should ideally be a reflection of God on the earth so others can see what He looks like.

Nevertheless, because of the curse of sin and death that came through Adam's rebellion, God's image in us was marred. Imagine seeing yourself in a mirror that has been shattered.

That is what Adam's sin did to us: It distorted our true image.

*And so it is written, "The first man Adam became a living being."[1] The last Adam became a life-giving spirit. …The first man was of the earth, made of dust; the second Man is the Lord from heaven. As was the man of dust, so also are those who are made of dust; and as is the heavenly Man, so also are those who are heavenly. And as we have borne the image of the man of dust, we shall also bear the image of the heavenly Man.* (1 Corinthians 15:45-49)

We see here that before Christ, we *were* a reflection of the first Adam: weak, rebellious, proud, and under sin's curse. Not a pretty picture, wouldn't you agree? But we *now* have a new image, we are a reflection of the "last Adam," Jesus the Christ: powerful, obedient to God's will, humble, and under God's Blessing.

## "We were designed to be the mirror image of God."

*…Where the Spirit of the Lord is, there is liberty. But we all, with unveiled face, beholding as in a mirror the glory of the Lord, are being transformed into the same image from glory to glory, just as by the Spirit of the Lord.* (2 Corinthians 3:17, 18)

Now think about that shattered mirror being restored to brand new: all the broken pieces fused back together supernaturally. Jesus came to do just that. God's perfect plan is for us to be "conformed to the image of His Son."[2]

To be just like Christ is the aim of the real Christian and God's destiny for us as His family. Jesus put all the broken pieces of the mirror back together and restored it to brand new.

We are transformed into His same image through thinking in a new way—God's way. This means that we see ourselves and our situations in light of the truth of God's Message,[3] the Bible, and yield to His Spirit in us.

Jesus gets the glory when we are an accurate picture of the freedom that He paid for us to receive.

## EMANCIPATION PROCLAMATION

We'll never see real freedom in our lives until we exchange our image of ourselves for God's image of us. To illustrate my point, think of the slaves after slavery was abolished in America.

The truth is, the majority of slaves that were declared free by the President's Emancipation Proclamation continued to live as slaves. Why? Because they never *saw* themselves as free.

They chose to continue to live on the plantations because they couldn't imagine any other possibilities. Similarly, until we change the image of ourselves and make it line up with how God sees us, our circumstances will never change.

## *"We'll never see real freedom in our lives until we exchange our image of ourselves for God's image of us."*

Most of us are trying to change ourselves by beginning with the external things we don't like—such as our behavior. True change has to come from the inside. It's not until you deal with the *roots* of the problem that you will see the fruits of the problem change too.

Think of someone who has always been poor. One day he or she wins a multi-million dollar lottery. Do you realize what the odds are that they will remain rich? Slim to none.

I will say it this way: poor thinking leads to poor living. If you see yourself as poor, then you'll always be poor. On the other hand, if you see yourself as rich, in due course, your circumstances will match your inward vision.

The self-image we have determines our behavior in life. Where does it begin? How is our self-image formed? It is shaped by the words we hear starting from the time we were born.

The words we hear from parents, siblings, "friends," etc. either build us up or tear us down. Our own words about ourselves have an even greater impact on our self-esteem.

In fact, God tells us through Proverbs that our *words* are matters of life and death.[6] Our words frame our world.

When we hear ourselves say things like, "You're worthless," "You're stupid," "You're helpless," etc. then our expectations of ourselves become lower and lower. Our God-given potentials are not realized.

Recognize this: not all the voices you hear in your head come from you. Some are from the enemy.

Because I never knew that fact, I would say, or give voice to, whatever I heard in my head. The image I had of myself was a porno addict, a slave to my own desires: weak, sinful, and helpless to change.

Then the Spirit of God gave me a new picture of myself as I studied the Word of God. I learned that I was "more than a conqueror through Him who loved [me]," [4] and that God "always leads [me] to triumph in Christ." [5]

Through personalizing the scriptures, such as the ones I just cited, I began to see that the Bible was God talking to me, to *me* personally. I used the imagination God gave me to begin seeing myself as a champion, not a loser; as a victor not a victim. And so should you.

The problem of lust is bigger than you and me, but it is definitely *not* bigger than God. God lives in us through faith in Christ. [7,8] It is up to us to make this adjustment in the way we think. God will not do it for us, but He helps us do it by giving us His Word as a tool to fix what is broken.

> **"I used the imagination God gave me to begin seeing myself as a champion, not a loser; as a victor not a victim."**

Look at this verse from Romans, "Don't copy the behavior and customs of this world, but let God transform you into a new person by changing the way you think. Then you will learn to know God's will for you, which is good and pleasing and perfect."[3]

Notice in this verse that the responsibility is not on God to change the way we think, but on *us*. Transformation in life happens as we change our thought process to line up with what God says.

Using God's Word as our weapon, we *can* take every thought captive that contradicts God and bring that thought into obedience to Him. The first step to accomplishing this is to make His Word the *final authority* in your life.

## DEAD MAN WALKING

Imagine for a moment that you are at a co-worker's funeral. This man was always chasing women while he was alive. A strange thing happens during the memorial service. Someone bends down and says to the corpse inside the casket, "Hey, Joe, check out all the hot women who came to your funeral." Do you think Joe is going to sit up and look around? Of course not! Because Joe is *dead*. Joe cannot be tempted, because dead men cannot give in to temptation.

Well, I have news for you. When we were made alive in Christ, our body—that which is tempted—died. Listen to this, "My old self has been crucified with Christ.

## *"...dead men cannot give in to temptation."*

It is no longer I who live, but Christ lives in me. So I live in this earthly body by trusting in the Son of God, who loved me and gave himself for me."[7]

We need to *see* ourselves as dead. That is where the challenge is. Your body does not know it is dead. You have to make sure it remembers. Consider yourself to be dead to sin, but alive to God in Christ Jesus.[8] The real question is, "How shall we who died to sin live any longer in it?"[9]

## CLEAN OUT YOUR CLOSET

Think about this: If you had old clothes in your closet that didn't fit, would you keep them? Would you try to still wear them? What if it was your favorite outfit? Just looking at it brings back memories that make you feel so good inside.

The majority of us are doing this very thing in the spiritual realm. Before we received Jesus as our Lord, we used to wear sin without any shame. We used to "strut our stuff" in our clothes that we thought were so cool, didn't we? We used to eat, drink, and even sleep in the same outfit. Before long we started to *stink*.

Then, when Jesus came into our lives and took His rightful place on the throne of our hearts, He cleaned us up and took the sinful rags away. He also gave us new clothes to wear. Royal robes which signified that we are now part of His family—His precious sons and heirs to His Kingdom!

Yet we have the nerve to try to fit into our old clothes. We still want to identify with them. The truth is that they don't fit us anymore. Those sinful rags keep us from moving freely in the spirit. They keep us from looking our best before God and others. Sin keeps us stuck in the past and it prevents us from moving on in life.

Our Father God has told us to put off the old person we used to be and put on the new person that we are in Christ.[10] That is what renewing our mind with God's perfect image of us is really all about. We need to clean out our closet of all of the old ways we used to think, talk, and act, and put on the new ways in which God wants us to think, talk, and act.

When God looks at us, He no longer sees the person we used to be. He sees the new creation we are *in Christ*. That means that He sees Jesus in us. We may look like an ordinary man on the outside, but we really look like God on the inside. Think about that!

## MAGNIFY GOD, NOT THE PROBLEM

Our God wants us to have a new vision for our lives and see new possibilities for ourselves. The truth is: with God, *all* things are possible for us who dare to believe.[11]

A perfect illustration of this is when the nation of Israel was told by the Lord God that they would possess another nation's land by first conquering the people who lived there. All of Israel became afraid when the Jewish spies brought back a bad report of giants and a superior military. God already said it was theirs and they still said it couldn't be done.[12]

They focused on the problem and it became so big in their minds that they thought it could never be overcome. The Bible says that they saw themselves as weak, small, and unable to accomplish God's plan.

However, there were two men with them who stood their ground and declared they *would* go and take the land because the Lord was with them. Among that whole generation, only two men & their families ended up possessing what the Lord desired for everyone in Israel.

## "Our God wants us to have a new vision for our lives."

Make a commitment today that you will be a man who says in the face of a seemingly impossible situation like this, "I will take what God has given me, and have my victory." The problem of lust becomes so *small* and easily overcome when we focus on how *big* our God is. He wants you to *possess* what Jesus *provided*. Let's do it!

## Let's Review

1. What is at the heart of the issue of overcoming lust?

2. Do you agree that your self-image is the biggest problem you face? Why or why not?

3. Whose instructions should we start with in life? Why?

4. What do you believe it means to be created in God's image?

5. What is God's destiny for us as Christians? Do you believe this destiny is attainable? Why or why not?

6. How is Jesus glorified in our life?

7. How do we deal with the fruit of the problem of lust? What are some practical ways we can do this?

8. How has your self-image been shaped into what it is now?

9. What have we used our imagination for? What *should* we use it for?

10. How have we seen ourselves? How should we see ourselves?

# NOTES:

_____

_____

_____

_____

_____

_____

_____

_____

_____

_____

_____

_____

_____

_____

_____

_____

_____

_____

_____

_____

_____

_____

_____

_____

_____

_____

_____

_____

_____

# THREE

# FRAMING YOUR WORLD

## CHANGING OUR COURSE

Now that we know that we need to see ourselves the way God sees us, the next question we need to answer is "how?" How do we take the image we have on the inside and apply it on the outside?

As I said in the last chapter, our self-image is built, demolished and rebuilt by *words*. Words are the building materials of our lives. They are as important as the framework is to a house when it is being constructed. Everything else hangs on them and is held together by them.

Other people's words have a large part to play in how we see ourselves. In addition, what you have *said* about yourself has shaped the way you *see* yourself, either for better or worse. Finally, God's words have the greatest impact on the image we have of ourselves when we take them as they are—the final authority on what is true and what is a lie.

## *"Words are the building materials of our lives."*

There is an event on TV called "The World's Strongest Man." A man from that competition by the name of Dave Gauder, who holds 17 world records for strength, was harnessed to a 66 ton train car. He actually pulled it along the train tracks in York, England.

It is simply amazing to read about a man moving such a huge piece of machinery. It is even more amazing to understand that a little muscle called the tongue has the power to steer our entire lives. *That is how crucial our words are.*

Think about an ocean liner. This huge sea vessel is kept on course by a relatively little piece of metal called the "rudder."

## *"What you have said about yourself has shaped the way you see yourself."*

Or consider a "bit" in a horse's mouth. By it, the rider can direct the horse exactly where he wants it to go. In the same way, God has designed our tongues with the purpose of keeping us on His course for our lives and taking us in His intended direction.[1]

## GOD'S SUCCESS SECRET

What if… you could have one of the wealthiest investors in the world as your personal mentor? Imagine that he has promised to give you the secret to his success in business. Would you pay close attention to every word he said? I would.

Well, thankfully, we have *the* most successful investor of all time mentoring us: God. He has invested *everything* He had in us through Jesus—and He expects a return on that investment. He tells us plainly how to be successful in overcoming lust:

*"Never stop reciting these teachings. You must think about them night and day so that you will faithfully do everything written in them. Only then will you prosper and succeed".* (Joshua 1:8 God's Word Translation)

**"God has designed our tongues with the purpose of keeping us on His course for our lives and taking us in His intended direction."**

Another way of saying that is: keep God's words continually in your mouth, think about them all the time, be looking to do what He says and then you will make your way successful. You are in control of your success in overcoming lust, not God. That may shock some of you, but it is true.

God plainly says in this passage of scripture that our success is up to *us*, not Him. Clearly, He *wants* us to be successful, just like any good father wants the best for his kids. Our success, however, depends on how well we obey His instructions and how well we follow His example.

## How It All Began

Turn to Genesis 1 and you'll see how God created the world we live in. First He spoke it, and then He saw it. He did what He did on purpose. He did not just throw some cosmic goo on the canvas of the universe and create everything haphazardly. He put things in order. He had the image firmly established inside Himself before He spoke, and then that image became reality through His words.

Now if *we* were with God "in the beginning" we would have probably said, "Wow, look how dark it is around here." Instead, God said, "Light." He didn't talk about what He saw. He talked about what He wanted to see. In other words, He didn't talk the problem. He talked the solution.

The Bible puts it this way, "God… calls those things which do not exist as though they did."[2] This is how the faith of God works. Could it be that God did this to show us how we need to operate in our daily situations?

Most of us quickly respond, "I could *never* do what God does. After all, He is *God*." He is: no doubt about that. And yet, He also told us to *imitate* Him just as children imitate their father.[3]

My daughter is constantly saying and doing things that she has heard me say or seen me do. Children are a reflection of their parents. They copy what they see and hear. Similarly, we were birthed by God's Spirit so that we can be a reflection of our Heavenly Father.

## LIKE FATHER, LIKE SON

Jesus had a lot to say about the importance of words. He revealed that they overflow from what our hearts are already filled with.

*"For whatever is in your heart determines what you say. A good person produces good things from the treasury of a good heart, and an evil person produces evil things from the treasury of an evil heart. And I tell you this, you must give an account on judgment day for every idle word you speak. The words you say will either acquit you or condemn you."* (Matthew 12:34-37, NLT)

The Master showed us how we can produce what we want to see in our lives: use our words as a carpenter would use their tools to build something useful out of a plain ol' hunk of wood. If we want to *see* good *things*, we need to *speak* good *words*. Our words should be working *for* us, not against us. Jesus says that we will be accountable for our "idle" words.

> ## "If we want to see good things, we need to speak good words."

Lazy, unproductive employees would get fired by any boss who was serious about the "bottom line," right? In the same way, we must dismiss *all* of the words we have been saying that have been producing nothing in our lives or—worse yet—producing bad things.

## Freedom NOW

How do we apply this to our lust situation? Instead of saying that we are slaves to our sexual appetite, we need to start saying that we *are* free from the bondage of lust. We are not *going to be* free one day, or when we get to heaven. We are free *now*. Do you see the distinction?

We are free *now* because Jesus has set us free. He provided our freedom through His death and resurrection. He already *has* delivered us from the power of darkness, including lust.[4] What happens in the present is that we simply receive by faith what Jesus has already provided. The same is true of salvation.

# *"It is from God's Word that we get the image of ourselves as being free. As we declare we are free, we'll see that freedom become a reality."*

It's already been given as a free gift because Jesus already paid for it. Now it's up to us to receive it, to take hold of it, and to own it.

It is from God's Word that we get the image of ourselves as being free. "*So if the Son liberates you [makes you free men], then you are really and unquestionably free.*" (John 8:36, AMP)

God's Word declares that if we believe in what Jesus did for us, we have been unquestionably set free through our faith in Him. We need to simply say the same thing God has already said about us.

Just as He spoke what He wanted to see during creation, He also said we *are* free in Christ Jesus.

As we declare the same freedom God declares over us, we will begin to see that freedom become an unquestionable reality in our lives. Call those things that do not yet exist as though they already did. Call "light" out of darkness. Like Father, like son. Instead of talking about how weak we are to overcome sexual temptation, we say, "I am strong in the Lord and in the power of *His* might." God says, "Let the weak *say*, 'I am strong.'"[5]

What helped me see my situation differently was the revelation that Jesus was tempted in every way, just as I am, yet He remained without sin.[6] Furthermore, I came to understand that Jesus is now living in me by His Spirit, because I have put my faith in Him. Therefore, *I* can remain without sin when facing temptation.

> **"It's not enough to have faith. You have to do something with it. Otherwise, it becomes weak and ineffective; like a flabby muscle."**

I started talking differently about myself and my situation. I began to say God's words like: "I am more than a conqueror through Christ.[7] I can do all things through Him making me strong.[8] Greater is He that lives in me than He that lives in the world.[9] This is the victory that overcomes the world and its lust: my *faith*."[10]

## Spiritual Exercises

Just like going to the gym and exercising our bodies, we can't expect results right away. We want to look in the mirror after our first work out and see if our muscles are any more noticeable. That is wishful thinking.

However, as you stay focused and stick with it, you will meet your physical goals. At first you feel like a fool to even try to work out. You will be tempted to think everyone else is looking at you like you're crazy.

It works the same way in the Kingdom of God. Faith comes by hearing God's Word *continually*. It is like gulping down an energy drink for your spirit. On the other hand, it's not enough to *have* faith. You have to *do* something with it. Otherwise, it becomes weak and ineffective; like a flabby muscle.

Speaking God's Word gets it in your heart, and acting on it makes you strong in the spirit. We will talk more on the action part of faith in the next chapter.

My point is: keep exercising your spirit with diligence. Do what your trainer, God's own Holy Spirit, is telling you to do and you will see results.

Get a hold of this powerful truth: changing our lives begins with changing our words. Jesus said that the good things and bad things we see in our lives can be traced back to our words.[11]

If you want to deal with the bad fruit that you see in your life, it won't do you any good to just snip off the branch that the fruit is hanging from; you have to go to the roots of the tree. By dealing with the root you'll deal with the fruit. Change the seeds of your words and you'll see different fruits produced in your life.

Proverbs tells us that the words we speak are actually a matter of life and death.[12] They really are *that* important. What have you been saying about yourself? What about your situation? Know this: you will *have* whatever you *say*.

## Let's Review

1. Do you see your course in life as set by you or by God?

2. What are three things, found in Joshua 1:8, which affect our success in life?

3. How are we to imitate God as our Father? See Romans 4:17 and Genesis 1 for clues.

4. According to Jesus, how do we produce good things in our lives?

5. When will you be free of lust?

6. How did Jesus overcome temptation in Luke 4?

7. Can we expect to remain without sin when we face temptation? Why or why not?

8. Should we expect to see results right away when we start making changes in our lives?

9. How does faith come?

10. Why are words so important?

## NOTES:

_____

_____

_____

_____

_____

_____

_____

_____

_____

_____

_____

_____

_____

_____

_____

_____

_____

_____

_____

_____

_____

_____

_____

_____

_____

_____

# FOUR

# THE NEW PLAYBOOK

## FOCUSING ON PURITY

In this chapter, we will be discussing practical guidelines that will help you reign over lust every day. When sports teams have their practice, it is usually a lot tougher than the action they see in the big game. This helps them stay prepared to face their opponents and win. In the same way, we need to be diligent and disciplined so that we will remain champions in life.

Previously, we learned that lust is waiting to put its hook into us when we take that second look at the person we are attracted to. When the temptation to look again hits you: be diligent to refuse its bait.

What I've trained my eyes to do is to look elsewhere after I first notice an appealing woman. For example, if I am in line at the store and some voluptuous female walks by, I will turn my neck and focus on the candy display at the register— *anything* else to shift my attention away from temptation.

Now, if you're *walking* and you notice someone you want to "feast your eyes on," my example can be dangerous. Don't focus on the floor and run into a wall, okay?

But seriously, you *can* refocus your attention on something else. With God's help, you can train your eyes to look where you direct them to look.

## *"Guarding our hearts should be a priority in our lives."*

I want to be clear: you have to be *intentional* to win against the strategies of lust. So, I have made a covenant with my eyes not to look on a woman lustfully. What that means is you do not let your *eyes* be your master; you make them your *servant*.

## GUARDING YOUR HEART

Your eyes and ears are the entrances to your heart. Look at what God says:

*"My son, pay attention to my words. Open your ears to what I say. Do not lose sight of these things. Keep them deep within your heart because they are life to those who find them and they heal the whole body. Guard your heart more than anything else, because the source of your life flows from it."* (Proverbs 4:20-23, God's Word Translation)

Notice God says open your ears to His words and don't lose sight of them. It goes on to say that this is the way God's Word is kept deep in your heart.

Guarding our hearts should be a priority in our lives. Think about military conquests. Armies that have walled cities are nearly impossible to conquer because they have several advantages.

First, they have excellent lookout points that help them see the enemy coming from miles away. Secondly, they can fire a long range attack that ends the enemy's plans before those plans can even begin. Lastly, assuming the enemy does somehow get close enough to start scaling the city's high walls, the defending army has a superior vantage point from which they can wage close combat. It is far easier to win when the enemy is underneath you.

### *"Don't let lust sabotage you by when it tries an all-out assault on your senses."*

So pay careful attention to what you are allowing into your heart.

Don't let lust sabotage you when it tries an all-out assault on your senses. It may look like a full-figure babe waiting to seduce you on the cover of that video, but inside the box is a bomb waiting to explode.

It may seem like a little innocent flirting with your co-worker, but it will lead to hurt and heartache. Learn to see it as the *trap* it really is so you won't take the bait.

I've changed what I link together with the temptation of lust. Instead of thinking about the immediate pleasure it brings like I used to, I now think about how my indulgence will hurt my relationship with Jesus, my best friend. I also think about the damage it will do to my marriage, my kids, my reputation, and my ministry.

With God's help, I've learned to associate guilt, shame, and condemnation with the temptation that lust throws at me. Even more importantly, I've come to associate my Father God being proud of me, my wife being able to trust me, my kids being confident in me, etc. with making the right choices.

I've learned that lust is a lot like a fire. The more you feed it, the more out of control it will become.

But if you starve lust, it will eventually burn out and die.

That means we have to vigilantly guard what we are putting in our eyes and ears because that is what fills our hearts. In other words, don't add fuel to lust's fire. Shut off and cut off anything or anyone that is feeding that lust addiction.

Guarding your heart means guarding what you allow in your *eyes* and *ears*.

A practical way I have done this is not wasting my time on entertainment that has sexually explicit content in it— visually OR audibly. That weeds out 80% of media for me. And, it also eliminates the majority of temptation in my life. It *seemed* hard in the beginning, but I am so glad I did it. It was a very wise decision—similar to an alcoholic who avoids going to bars, and I owe my pastor at that time who inspired me to do it a debt of thanks.

## MENTAL STRONGHOLDS

The second step we take in God's Playbook for winning against lust is controlling what we think about. Many think that is impossible to do, and, because they believe that, they put up roadblocks on their road to recovery.

If you dare to believe that it is not only possible to control your thoughts—but it is also God's command, then you will see your whole life change.

*"Fix your thoughts on what is true, and honorable, and right, and pure, and lovely, and admirable. Think about things that are*

*excellent and worthy of praise.*" (Philippians 4:8, New Living Translation)

That sums it up perfectly. Imagine setting a thermostat where you live. Once you set it, you just forget about it. You don't make it 76, then 92, then 64 every couple of minutes. You set it and keep it set. That's what we *must* do with our minds. *Set* them on what God says and keep them set.

Be like those big, tough bouncers at the club. Don't let any thought that is not on the list of God's promises come in the door of your mind. They'll only cause trouble. If one or two do manage to sneak in, kick them out.

Use the most powerful weapon there is: the spoken Word of God, the Sword of the Spirit.[1] Use it to pull down the strongholds that the enemy has crafted in your mind. Put that sword to the throat of the evil thoughts which arise, take them captive and make them obey Christ.[2]

Notice I said the *spoken* Word of God. A sword on display behind glass is of no threat to anyone. It needs to be in your hands to be effective against your opponent.

> ### "Use the most powerful weapon there is... and pull down the strongholds that the enemy has made in your mind."

God's Word is most effective when it is in your *mouth*. The Master demonstrated this principle when He was tempted.

Jesus responded to every deception the enemy threw at Him by quoting God's Word. He didn't just reject the deceptive thought; He replaced it with the truth.[3]

Let's do an exercise: Say you're on the road driving to work, and you stop at a red light. You happen to glance to the left, and there's a huge billboard with a woman on a bikini. The light turns green and you start driving. As you go, your mind is still thinking about the woman on bikini. It is at this point that you quickly recognize the bait.

I want you to say this part aloud with me: "I reject that thought and refuse to allow it to stay on my mind. I thank You Lord for this day. This is the day that You have made and I rejoice and am glad in it. Thank You for this car that runs. Thank You for my job and for giving me the ability to work. Thank you for clothes to wear and food to eat. Thank You, most of all, for loving me. Help me be effective in what I have to do today, in Jesus' name. Amen."

If you did the above exercise with me, you would have noticed that when you started speaking, the lingering thought did not stay there. It was replaced with the words that were coming out of your mouth.

This is how the Word of God becomes a sword that is used to cut the enemy to pieces, and how you can have authority over lust.

Notice that you have to open your mouth and say some things in order for you to gain the victory. Just like you can't win any game by being on the sidelines, you also must use the authority God has given you and *speak* in order to overcome the thoughts lust throws at you.

Words have power over our thoughts. That's how we can win. Change your thinking by changing your words. As you change your thinking you will also change your life.

## WISDOM'S WALLS

Next, we can change our actions by putting a perimeter of barriers around ourselves that keep us from making bad choices. For example, I decided to only surf the Internet at a public library, or at an "internet café" where anyone passing by can see what I'm looking at. I did this because I knew I couldn't trust myself to stay out of pornographic websites. I built walls that kept me away from doing something foolish that I would later regret.

There are now a few software packages that will help you stay clean from the lust "drug." Some filter the websites that have explicit content so you don't open that e-door. Another option is called "Covenant Eyes," in which you can have someone that you trust find out where you were online. This way, you have accountability which inspires you to stay away from the wrong websites.

It is critical to establish barriers in your relationships, too. My wife and I decided before we got married that we wanted our first kiss to be on our wedding day.

Most people think this is a very noble but lofty goal: one that's next to impossible to realize. Both of us had been very intimate physically with the people we had dated previously. So we knew we had to set up very strict guidelines that would keep us from going "out of bounds."

## "There are no 'accidents' when it comes to staying pure OR messing up sexually, I assure you."

We did this by choosing to only date at public places. We would only watch a movie if someone else "chaperoned" us. No conversations behind closed doors either, except on the phone. We also kept the physical touch to a minimum. In fact, we didn't even hold hands or hug until we were already courting for six months.

This may sound extreme. I remember my wife's cousin being so frustrated with the two of us because we were almost icy in terms of physical affection. But it was because we knew it only took a spark to get a forest fire going. And we also knew our own weaknesses all too well.

You can decide to drive somewhere without using a roadmap. I know people who have tried, myself included, only to end up lost or frustrated most of the time. In the same way, we *must* use the roadmap of God's wisdom to arrive at our intended destination of purity.

I wouldn't say it was "easy" for my wife and I to reach our goal, by any stretch of the imagination. Yet, we are thankful that we charted our course and got back on track when we took a wrong turn. And yes, we did realize the goal of having our first kiss on our wedding day! When you set up these kinds of boundaries in your life, you will be effective in keeping yourself safe.

What would cause us to do this? Our motivation for all of this must be that of pleasing God. Encourage yourself to steer as far as possible from temptation. This way, you don't allow yourself to get pulled back into the past.

There are no "accidents" when it comes to staying pure *or* messing up sexually. People don't plan to fail, they fail to plan. Ask God to help you develop a plan that gives you specific boundaries that you know you shouldn't cross.

## WALK IN THE LIGHT

You'll remember in the first chapter I pointed out that lust wants you to cover up your addiction and pretend that it doesn't exist. Well, this means that in order to keep lust under your heel where it belongs, you should do just the opposite.

I tell people I've known for years and even total strangers about the prison that lust had made of my life and how wonderful it is to be free now, thanks to Jesus and the help of the Holy Spirit. I do this deliberately to keep myself out in the open, in the light of God's grace and truth.

In other words, expose lust before it exposes you. Don't fall into the trap of thinking it's *all* because of your efforts once you start experiencing victory.

## "God's best is for us to be free from lust and live victoriously through Christ."

Point others to the power that comes from Jesus to change lives. Your testimony about how God has changed *your* life cannot be argued with.

# A FULL Life

I don't want to imply by what I've written so far that overcoming lust is simply a matter of do's and don'ts. This is not about being legalistic. Following Jesus as our Lord means that our lives revolve around our relationship with Him.

The strategies this book has given you in overcoming lust cannot be successful for the long term without filling your life up with Jesus. Just as it is with everyone else we associate with in life, the depth of our friendship will be determined by how much time we spend together in meaningful communication.

It is critical that we *make time* to talk with our Lord each day, throughout the day. Every time I open my Bible, I remind myself that my closest friend is speaking to me from the pages I'll read. I urge you to do the same.

The more we interact with Him, the more we charge our spiritual "batteries" with His love, and the more armed and dangerous we are in facing the temptations lust throws at us.

Lust tries to sell us a *counterfeit*. Lust wants us to believe that a few minutes of pleasure should be picked over the eternal pleasure of Jesus saying "Well done." The more our relationship with Jesus is growing and thriving, the less we have time and a desire to pursue anything but being closer to Him.

## A Final Thought

I'll leave you with this to chew on: our decisions determine our destination. Our decisions will determine whether or not we fulfill God's destiny for us. God's best is for us to be free from lust and live victoriously through Christ. Don't settle for less than God's best. It's just not worth it.

Get on the right path, and stay on it. Rely on God's help to keep you focused on what you want: on your goal to be truly free just like Jesus wanted you to be, enjoying life "to the fullest." The choices we make determine the life we'll have. Good choices, good life. God says, "I have set before you life and death, blessing and cursing… choose this day whom you will serve." It is no longer God's choice; it is *your choice*. Which path will you choose?

# LET'S REVIEW

1. Do you believe it is possible to train your eyes to look elsewhere when facing the temptation to lust?

2. Why is it important to guard our eyes and ears?

3. Write down some things that feed the fire of lust in your life. Then write down ways you can cut off these things that fuel the fire.

4. How can we change our thinking? What else does our thinking affect?

5. Honestly, what competes with God's Word in your life in informing you what acceptable behavior is and what is not?

6. Have you set up boundaries in your personal life? In your love life? What were the results?

7. What should be our motivation in making these changes in our life?

8. Do you agree that there are no accidents in our sex life? Why or why not?

9. How do you plan to "let out" your secret about your lust addiction?

10. How do our decisions affect our destiny?

# NOTES:

_____

_____

_____

_____

_____

_____

_____

_____

_____

_____

_____

_____

_____

_____

_____

_____

_____

_____

_____

_____

_____

_____

_____

_____

_____

_____

_____

# FIVE

# How YOU Can Make A Difference

## Marching Orders

Now that you are on the road to renewing your mind where lust is concerned, I also want to let you know of some exciting opportunities you have to make a difference in the lives of others. I would say that 99.99% of men are struggling with this problem, and the other 0.01% are in denial.

Seriously though, the joy that you experience walking in freedom and victory over lust can be multiplied exponentially as you help other men get a hold of the truth you just learned.

## Word of Mouth

We have a powerful influence as we spread the word about our new-found freedom. So much in our society happens based on making our voices heard.

Media is so effective because it uses several avenues to make its message heard. The more we hear it, the more we believe it. God is the One who originally said so.[1] Usually those with the loudest voices are the ones who bring changes to political policies, social reforms, etc. We who now know the truth must make *our* voices heard so that others can also experience their freedom.

If this book has benefited you, please let others know. Together, we can and *must* make a difference by recommending it to others, giving it as a gift, sending out blogs and emails about it, etc.

## Share in the Reward

Partnership is another way you can make a huge impact on the world around you that has been eaten up with the problem of lust and trapped in its lies. If one person made it their goal to get introduced to everyone on the planet, you would think they were nuts.

In the same way, I cannot reach everyone who needs to be reached all by myself. This vision God gave me of reaching every man who needs to know freedom from lust can only become a reality as we work together and each do our part. God said we are to partner with Him and each other in order to accomplish all the good He wants to see done in this world.

The first way you can partner with us is to pray. Prayer is a powerful way of seeing God accomplish what He wants to do on this earth. Jesus taught us to pray that God's will be done "on earth as it is in Heaven."

## *"As we share in another's labor, we partner with them and share their reward."*

There is no one imprisoned by lust in Heaven. I guarantee you that. God doesn't want us to be slaves to lust on earth either. When we pray and believe together that men would have the opportunity to hear this good news of freedom from lust through Christ, we will see it happen.

There is a second way for you to partner with us to see this vision become a reality. Jesus said that we can receive a reward even when we have not worked for it.[2] That sounds like a great deal to me. How is that possible?

As we share in another's labor, we partner with them and share their reward. I see this project as "seed" that is being sown in men's hearts, and I know that there is a reward of a big harvest of souls saved, healed, and set free. You can share in that reward.

Jesus, Paul, and others in the Bible operated on this same God-given principle in their ministries. Their work was financed by partners who believed in what they were doing and wanted to help support it. When we receive spiritually from someone, we should be inclined to give financially.[3]

The message of Jesus is free, but the means of communicating it is not. In other words, it takes money to print books, order promotional materials etc. I urge you to do this only as the Lord lays it on your heart. He loves it when we give *gladly*, not grudgingly or under compulsion.

My motivation in inviting you to become a partner is not in what I will receive, but in what *you'll* receive for your investment. When you sow generously, you also reap generously: a harvest of souls set free.

# NETWORKING

One way you can get started on partnering with this ministry is to introduce three friends or relatives to the mini-book you hold in your hands. Believe me; this won't be hard when you consider how many men are dealing with this problem, statistically speaking.

To help you keep yourself accountable to follow through on this assignment, I'm providing you space below to write their first names:

_____

_____

_____

# FOR FURTHER STUDY

Lastly, you can turn this mini-book into a discussion group or Bible Study. Invite a few guys you know, talk up the book to your friends, and then assign the chapters as "homework."

The next time you get together, go through the discussion questions listed at the end of the assigned chapter. I already did all of the hard work for you. Just make sure you have some type of food on hand. You know guys like to eat. Serve the spiritual food with the natural and enjoy!

# FOOTNOTES

## Chapter Two

[1] Genesis 2:7
[2] Romans 8:29
[3] Romans 12:2 NLT
[4] Romans 8:37
[5] 2 Corinthians 2:14
[6] Proverbs 18:21
[7] Galatians 2:20
[8] Romans 6:11
[9] Romans 6:2
[10] Ephesians 4:20-24
[11] Mark 9:23
[12] Numbers 13

## Chapter Three

[1] James 3:2-4

[2] Romans 4:17
[3] Ephesians 5:1
[4] Colossians 1:13
[5] Joel 3:10b
[6] Hebrews 4:15
[7] Romans 8:37
[8] Philippians 4:13
[9] 1 John 4:4
[10] 1 John 5:4
[11] Matthew 12:34-37
[12] Proverbs 18:21

## Chapter Four

[1] Ephesians 6:17
[2] 2 Corinthians 10:3-5
[3] Matthew 4:1-11

## Chapter Five

[1] Romans 10:17
[2] John 4:36-38
[3] 1 Timothy 5:17, 18

www.ingramcontent.com/pod-product-compliance
Lightning Source LLC
Chambersburg PA
CBHW020356290526
45785CB00005B/2315